Ecosystems
Polar Regions

Simon Rose

www.av2books.com

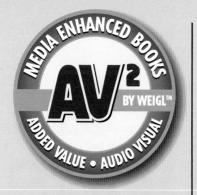

AV² provides enriched content that supplements and complements this book. Weigl's AV² books strive to create inspired learning and engage young minds in a total learning experience.

Your AV² Media Enhanced books come alive with...

Audio
Listen to sections of the book read aloud.

Key Words
Study vocabulary, and complete a matching word activity.

Go to **www.av2books.com,** and enter this book's unique code.

BOOK CODE

J573864

Video
Watch informative video clips.

Quizzes
Test your knowledge.

Embedded Weblinks
Gain additional information for research.

Slide Show
View images and captions, and prepare a presentation.

AV² by Weigl brings you media enhanced books that support active learning.

Try This!
Complete activities and hands-on experiments.

... and much, much more!

Published by AV² by Weigl
350 5th Avenue, 59th Floor
New York, NY 10118
Website: www.av2books.com   www.weigl.com

Library of Congress Cataloging-in-Publication Data
Rose, Simon, 1961-
 Polar Regions / Simon Rose.
    pages cm. -- (Ecosystems)
Includes index.
 ISBN 978-1-62127-486-5 (hardcover : alk. paper) -- ISBN 978-1-62127-489-6 (softcover : alk. paper)
1. Ecology--Polar regions--Juvenile literature. 2. Ice caps--Polar regions--Juvenile literature. 3. Polar regions--Juvenile literature. 4. Endangered ecosystems--Juvenile literature. I. Title.
 QH541.5.P6R67 2014
 577.0911'3--dc23
                                    2012046703

Printed in the United States of America in North Mankato, Minnesota
1 2 3 4 5 6 7 8 9 0 17 16 15 14 13

042013
WEP300113

Project Coordinator Aaron Carr
Design Mandy Christiansen

Every reasonable effort has been made to trace ownership and to obtain permission to reprint copyright material. The publishers would be pleased to have any errors or omissions brought to their attention so that they may be corrected in subsequent printings.

Photo Credits
Weigl acknowledges Getty Images as its primary photo supplier for this title.

Contents

AV² Book Code 2

What are Polar Region Ecosystems? 4

Where in the World? 6

Mapping Polar Regions 8

Polar Region Climates 10

Types of Polar Regions 12

Features of Polar Regions 13

Life in Polar Regions 14

Polar Region Plants 16

Polar Region Mammals 18

Polar Region Plankton, Birds,
and Invertebrates 20

Polar Regions in Danger 22

Science in the Polar Regions 24

Working in the Polar Regions 26

Make Seawater 28

Create a Food Web 29

Eco Challenge 30

Key Words/Index 31

Log on to www.av2books.com 32

What are Polar Region Ecosystems?

Due to the tilt of the Earth, the Sun never rises more than 23.5 degrees above the horizon at either pole.

Earth is home to millions of **organisms**. Each of these organisms depends on its environment and the other organisms around it for survival. These organisms interact with each other and the environment they live in. These interactions between organisms and their environments create **ecosystems**.

Polar regions are a type of ecosystem. The Arctic polar region is in the northern **hemisphere**, around the North Pole. In the southern hemisphere, the polar region is on the continent of Antarctica, around the South Pole. Polar region ecosystems are generally cold all year, even in summer.

The cold temperatures and harsh climate of polar ecosystems mean there are few animals and plants. The organisms that do live there have adapted to survive in the extreme climate. Both northern and southern polar regions are isolated areas. Few humans live in the polar regions. Despite this, both regions face increasing environmental threats from climate change and human activity.

Eco Facts

Polar region ecosystems are not as diverse as ecosystems in other parts of the world. However, they are home to different types of animals, fish, birds, plants, and marine organisms.

Levels of Organization in Polar Region Ecosystems

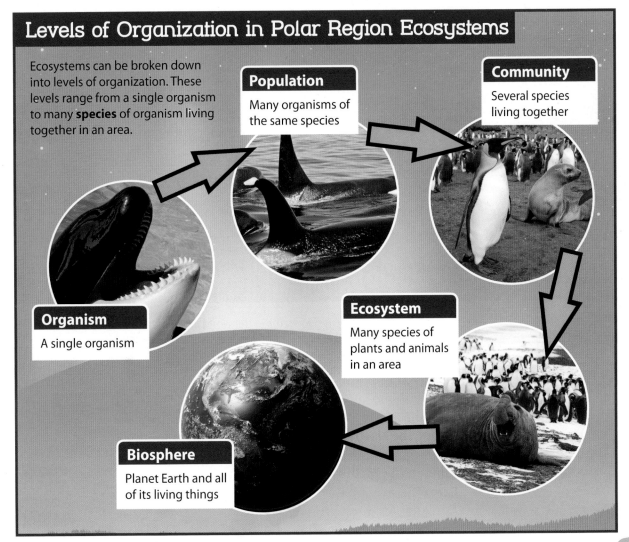

Ecosystems can be broken down into levels of organization. These levels range from a single organism to many **species** of organism living together in an area.

Population
Many organisms of the same species

Community
Several species living together

Organism
A single organism

Ecosystem
Many species of plants and animals in an area

Biosphere
Planet Earth and all of its living things

Where in the World?

Some of the largest icebergs in the world are in the Antarctic. Penguins and seals may use icebergs for shelter or as resting places.

The North Pole is the northernmost point on the Earth. It is located in the middle of Arctic Ocean. There is no land at the North Pole. Instead, the North Pole is covered with constantly shifting sea ice for most of the year. Scientists believe that within the next few decades, the North Pole may become ice-free in summer as a result of climate change. This may open up the **Northwest Passage**. The South Pole is the southernmost point on the Earth's surface. It is located on land on the continent of Antarctica. Many areas around the two poles also have polar climates. Generally, these areas lie within the Arctic and Antarctic Circles.

The Arctic and Antarctic Circles are lines of **latitude** drawn on maps of Earth. The Arctic Circle runs through territory controlled by Norway, Sweden, Finland, Russia, the United States, Canada, Iceland, and Denmark. The Arctic Circle also crosses Greenland, which is the world's largest island. Greenland contains some of the world's largest areas of ice. In the south, the continent of Antarctica occupies much of the area within the Antarctic Circle. No single country controls Antarctica. It is used for scientific research by many nations.

Eco Facts

Antarctica is very cold, and most water on the continent is frozen. The ice in Antarctica contains about 70 percent of Earth's fresh water.

Keeping time can be a problem for people who work at the poles. Time zones were invented to help keep accurate time around the world. At the poles, all time zones meet and no official time zone has been assigned. Also, time keeping is related to the position of the Sun, such as noon happening when the Sun is overhead. Due to the tilt of the Earth on its axis, at both poles the Sun rises once in the spring and then does not set until winter. People working at the North and South Poles often set the time based on where they are from, or based on an agreed upon time zone.

Establishing direction can be a problem in the polar regions, as well. At the North Pole, all directions point south. At the South Pole, all directions point north. This is due to Earth's **magnetic field.** This can make travel difficult for the scientists working at the poles.

Several species of penguins make their homes in Antarctica. No penguins live in the Arctic polar regions.

Mapping Polar Regions

This map shows some of the important areas in the polar regions. Find the place where you live on the map. Do you live close to a polar region? If not, which polar region is closest to you?

ARCTIC OCEAN

NORTH AMERICA

ATLANTIC OCEAN

EQUATOR

PACIFIC OCEAN

SOUTH AMERICA

SOUTHERN OCEAN

Legend

■ Polar Regions

▪ ▪ Northwest Passage

▨ Land

▢ Ocean

∿ River

Scale at Equator

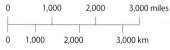

```
0        1,000    2,000    3,000 miles

0    1,000    2,000    3,000 km
```

N

Southern Ocean

Location: Surrounding the continent of Antarctica

Area: 20.3 million square miles (52.6 million square kilometers)

Fact: The Southern Ocean is one of the stormiest oceans on Earth.

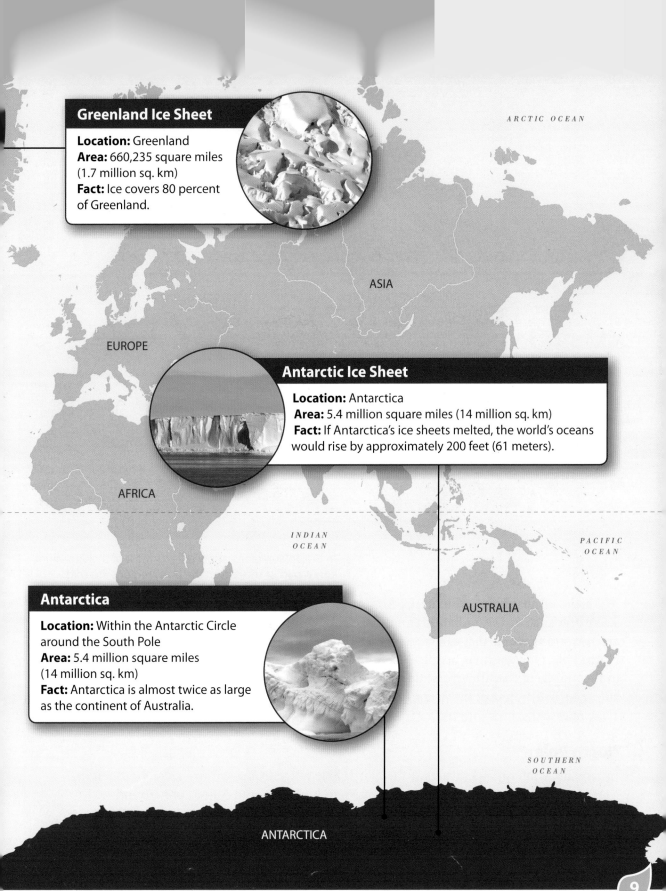

Greenland Ice Sheet

Location: Greenland
Area: 660,235 square miles
(1.7 million sq. km)
Fact: Ice covers 80 percent
of Greenland.

ARCTIC OCEAN

ASIA

EUROPE

Antarctic Ice Sheet

Location: Antarctica
Area: 5.4 million square miles (14 million sq. km)
Fact: If Antarctica's ice sheets melted, the world's oceans
would rise by approximately 200 feet (61 meters).

AFRICA

INDIAN
OCEAN

PACIFIC
OCEAN

Antarctica

Location: Within the Antarctic Circle
around the South Pole
Area: 5.4 million square miles
(14 million sq. km)
Fact: Antarctica is almost twice as large
as the continent of Australia.

AUSTRALIA

SOUTHERN
OCEAN

ANTARCTICA

Polar Region Climates

In the polar regions, snow reflects most of the Sun's light. This is part of the reason the polar regions are cold.

Earth's **atmosphere** is thin in the Arctic and Antarctic. As a result, the Sun's ultraviolet, or UV, radiation can cause sunburns within a few minutes. There are also strong winds that can create blizzards. The South Pole is colder than the North Pole. One reason is because the South Pole is located at a higher altitude in the middle of a continent, while the North Pole is at sea level in the middle of an ocean. The waters of the Arctic Ocean draw heat from the air in the summer. They release this heat into the air in winter.

North Pole

In January, winter temperatures at the North Pole range from –45° to –15° Fahrenheit (–43° to –26° Celsius). Summer temperatures in June, July, and August are around 32°F (0°C). In summer, there are 24 hours of daylight, with darkness returning at the start of winter. The sea ice at the North Pole is usually 6 to 10 feet (1.8 to 3 m) thick. This has recently decreased due to climate change.

South Pole

Antarctica is very large and its climate varies from place to place. Temperatures may be higher on some of the coasts and colder in the high mountains. Winter in Antarctica is from March to September. Summer is from September to March.

The average winter temperature is about −72°F (−58°C). In winter, the South Pole receives no sunlight. From about March to September, it is dark except for starlight and moonlight. The Sun reappears in September, signaling the start of 24 hours of daylight.

In January, it is midsummer at the South Pole. During this time, the temperature averages −15°F (−26°C). The highest temperature recorded at the South Pole was 59°F (15°C) in January 1974.

Eco Facts

The lowest temperature ever recorded on Earth is −128.6°F (−89.2°C). This was recorded on July 21, 1983 at Vostok Station, a Russian research base 808 miles (1,300 km) from the South Pole.

Cold Deserts

Though there is snow, the polar regions are very dry. Antarctica and much of the Arctic are actually deserts. Antarctica receives an average of only 6.5 inches (16.5 centimeters) of **precipitation** each year. Some areas of the Arctic only receive about 4 inches (10 cm) of precipitation.

In July, ships called icebreakers can often sail to the North Pole, breaking a path through the thinner summer ice.

Types of Polar Regions

Located in the polar regions are the polar ice caps. Ice caps may also be called glaciers. Ice caps are thick layers of ice that cover less than 19,000 square miles (42,000 sq. km). Ice sheets are thick areas of ice that cover more than 19,000 square miles (42,000 sq. km). A series of connected ice sheets and glaciers forms an ice field. The two main areas with ice sheets are Greenland and Antarctica.

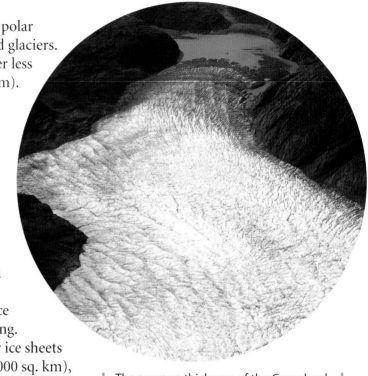

Greenland Ice Sheet

The Greenland ice sheet covers an area about three times the size of Texas. In recent years, however, the Greenland ice sheet has begun to shrink due to melting. The areas of Greenland not covered by ice sheets amount to 135,000 square miles (350,000 sq. km), which is about the size of Germany.

The average thickness of the Greenland ice sheet is 5,000 feet (1,524 m).

In some parts of Antarctica, the ice is more than 15,650 feet (4,770 m) thick.

Antarctic Ice Sheet

In the south, the Antarctic ice sheet covers the continent of Antarctica. It is Earth's biggest single mass of ice. The average thickness of the Antarctic ice sheet is 6,500 feet (1,981 m). Antarctica is the highest continent on Earth. Almost all of Antarctica is covered in ice sheets. The surface of these ice sheets is about 9,000 feet (2,743 m) above sea level. Together, the Greenland and Antarctic ice sheets contain more than 99 percent of the world's freshwater.

Features of Polar Regions

Icebergs

Icebergs are large chunks of ice that break off from glaciers or polar ice caps and float out to sea. About ninety percent of an iceberg's size is hidden below the surface. Antarctic icebergs generally are much bigger than Arctic icebergs. The largest iceberg ever recorded was 183 miles (295 km) long and more than 23 miles (37 km) wide.

Volcanoes

There are many volcanoes in Antarctica. Mount Erebus is the second highest volcano in Antarctica. This volcano is 12,448 feet (3,794 m) tall. It has erupted many times. Mount Sidley is the tallest volcano in Antarctica at 14,058 feet (4,285 m). It is **dormant**.

Midnight Sun and Polar Night

In summer, the Sun does not fully set at the poles. Around midsummer, the Sun may be visible in the sky at midnight. This is called the midnight Sun. In winter, the Sun never fully rises at the poles. It is dark for six months. When there is a polar day at the North Pole, it is polar night at the South Pole.

Aurora

This is a display of light that occurs around the polar regions when energy from the Sun hits the Earth. This energy is pulled to the polar regions by the Earth's magnetic field. Here, it reacts with the atmosphere. In the northern hemisphere, the lights are called the *aurora borealis,* or northern lights. In the southern hemisphere, they are called the *aurora australis*, or southern lights.

Life in Polar Regions

In polar region ecosystems, organisms depend on each other for the food, or energy, they need to survive. This energy transfers between organisms through the food chain.

Producers

The plant-like organisms found around the polar regions are producers for other organisms in the ecosystem. These organisms are called producers because they make their own food. Producers absorb energy from the Sun and convert it into usable forms of energy, such as sugar. This process is called photosynthesis. Producers found in polar regions include algae, plankton, and bacteria.

Primary Consumers

The animals that rely on producers for food are called primary consumers. When a primary consumer feeds on a producer, some of the energy made by the producer is transferred to the consumer. Examples of primary consumers found in polar region ecosystems include krill, cod, and squid.

Polar Region Energy Pyramid

The transfer of energy in an ecosystem begins with producers and moves up the energy pyramid to the tertiary consumers. Organisms at each level of the pyramid receive energy from the organisms in the levels below them.

Outside of the pyramid are the decomposers. They break down the dead and decaying **organic** matter left behind when plants and animals die. For this reason, decomposers receive energy from organisms in all levels of the energy pyramid.

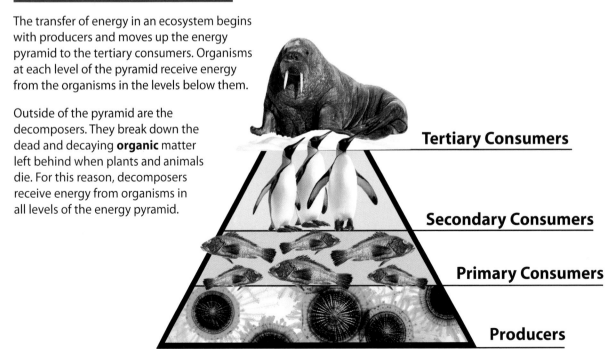

Tertiary Consumers

Secondary Consumers

Primary Consumers

Producers

Polar Region Food Web

Another way to study the flow of energy through an ecosystem is by examining food chains and food webs. A food chain shows how a producer feeds a primary consumer, which then feeds a secondary consumer, and so on. However, most organisms feed on many different food sources. This practice causes food chains to interconnect, creating a food web.

In this example related to a polar ecosystem, the **red** line represents one food chain from the plankton to the Arctic cod and the orca. The **blue** line from the algae to the krill, seal, and orca forms another food chain. These food chains connect at the orca, but they also connect in other places. The cod also feeds on algae, and the krill also eats plankton. This series of connections forms a complex food web.

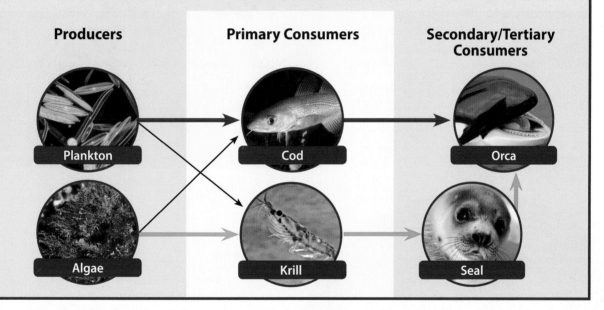

Secondary and Tertiary Consumers

Secondary consumers feed on both producers and primary consumers. Around polar regions, secondary consumers include seals, penguins, and some whales. Orcas in Antarctica and polar bears in the Arctic are called tertiary consumers. Tertiary consumers feed on secondary and primary consumers.

Decomposers

Small **crustaceans**, including shrimp, crabs, and many types of bacteria, live in polar region ecosystems. These organisms are decomposers. They eat dead and decaying organic materials, such as dead fish. Decomposers are then eaten by secondary and tertiary consumers.

Polar Region Plants

Despite the cold temperatures and short growing seasons, plants, algae, fungi, and lichens can be found in both the Arctic and Antarctic. The Arctic **tundra** has a layer of soil called **permafrost** that is frozen all year. About 1,700 plant species live in the tundra. These plants are usually very small and grow low to the ground. They also grow close together. Only a thin layer of soil thaws in the spring, so polar region plants have shallow root systems.

Arctic Plants

Arctic willow is a dwarf shrub that provides food for caribou, musk oxen, and Arctic hares. Bearberry is an evergreen plant with silky hairs and leathery leaves to protect it from the wind and cold. Purple saxifrage is one of the earliest tundra plants to bloom. It grows in a tight, low clump with tiny star-shaped flowers. The Arctic poppy grows 4 to 6 inches (10 to 15 cm) tall. It produces a single flower.

Arctic willow is the northernmost wood-producing plant in the world.

Lichens

Lichens grow at both poles. They are formed from a fungus and an alga. The fungus supplies water and minerals. The alga provides energy through photosynthesis. Lichens grow on rocks and on the ground. Their small size and slow growth help them survive in harsh environments, such as polar region ecosystems. Experiments have shown that lichen can survive in outer space for several weeks.

Some lichens in Antarctica have been dated to more than 5,300 years old.

Antarctic Hair Grass

Antarctic hair grass and Antarctic pearlwort are the two native plants in Antarctica. They grow in small clumps on the Antarctic **Peninsula** where there are warmer temperatures. Antarctica also has more than 300 species of non-marine algae, 300 different mosses, and around 150 types of lichens.

Antarctic hair grass is spreading along the Antarctic Peninsula. This is due to warmer summers caused by climate change.

Eco Facts

Thin soil and a short growing season prevent larger plants and trees from growing in polar regions. Climate change may affect this. As the climate warms, new kinds of plants may begin to grow in these regions.

Polar Region Mammals

There are no land mammals in Antarctica. In the Arctic, there are several land mammals, including the Arctic fox, the Arctic hare, and the polar bear. Both polar regions are home to many species of marine mammals, such as whales.

Polar Bear

Polar bears are the main Arctic land **predators**. Adult polar bears can weigh up to 1,500 pounds (680 kilograms). Their white coats provide camouflage as they hunt, as well as warmth in the cold climate.

Polar bears are strong swimmers and can stay underwater for two minutes at a time. They live on land, but in winter, polar bears go out to sea on the ice. There, they search for holes made in the ice by seals. When a seal comes up, the bear pulls it out of the water. In summer, they eat berries and vegetation.

Polar bears have longer legs and larger feet than other bears. This helps them walk on ice.

Walrus

Walruses are large marine mammals. They are found throughout the Arctic. There are two main species. The male Pacific walrus can weigh between 1,800 and 3,700 pounds (816 and 1,678 kg). The Atlantic species is smaller. Males of both species are larger than females. Both sexes have tusks, which they can use to fight and cut through ice. Excellent swimmers, walruses can dive up to 300 feet (91 m). They do so to feed on clams. They also eat fish, seals, and even young whales.

Walrus tusks are made of ivory. They average 1.6 feet (0.5 m) in length.

Humpback Whale

Humpbacks are baleen whales. Instead of teeth, these whales have baleen plates. They use these plates to filter food from the water. Baleen is made of keratin. This is the same material that makes up human fingernails and hair. Baleen looks like long strands of hair.

In summer, humpbacks feed on invertebrates, such as krill. They also eat plankton and small fish around the north and south polar regions. Humpback whales migrate to areas closer to the equator in winter. Humpback whales can live up to 100 years. Females average 49 to 52 feet (15 to 16 m) in length. Males tend to be slightly smaller than females. Humpbacks are known for their distinctive songs. Like some other types of whales, humpbacks often leap out of the water.

Eco Facts

Polar bears are threatened by climate change. Climate change is warming the polar regions. This is causing the polar ice caps to melt. Less ice will affect the polar bear's ability to hunt.

Orca

Also known as killer whales, orcas are found in all the world's oceans. Orcas have black and white coloring. The long fins that rise out of their backs, called dorsal fins, can be up to 6 feet (1.8 m) tall. Adult males grow to around 27 feet (8.2 m) long. Females are usually smaller. Calves are about 8 feet (2.4 m) long when they are born.

Orcas feed on fish, seals, walruses, and smaller whales. Their teeth are sharp and can grow up to 5 inches (12.7 cm) long. Orcas can swim at 25 miles (40 km) per hour. They are social animals and travel in groups called pods.

On average, an orca can remain underwater for 10 minutes before it must surface to breathe.

Polar Region Plankton, Birds, and Invertebrates

The waters of the polar regions are teeming with life. Many species of invertebrates and fish live in these waters. Birds, such as penguins, feed on these organisms.

Plankton

Plankton are tiny animals that currents, tides, and waves move through the world's oceans. Most types of plankton are too small to be seen. Some kinds of plankton, called phytoplankton, absorb energy from sunlight and minerals from seawater. They are the most common producers in polar ecosystems. Another kind of plankton, called zooplankton, serve as food for larger marine creatures, such as cod.

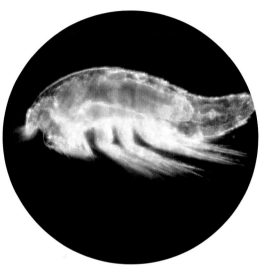

When Arctic zooplankton die, they fall to the ocean floor. Here, they are eaten by clams and other organisms.

Penguins

Antarctica is home to five major species of penguins. The Adélie penguin is the smallest, at about 27 inches (68.6 cm) tall and between 8.5 and 12 pounds (3.9 and 5.4 kg). The chinstrap penguin is the most numerous, with 12 to 13 million living in Antarctica. They are about 28 inches (71 cm) tall and weigh 9 to 14 pounds (4.1 to 6.4 kg). Emperor penguins stand 4 feet (1.2 m) tall and can weigh 70 to 80 pounds (32 and 36 kg). Penguins feed on krill and fish. The Galapagos penguin is the only species to live north of the equator in nature. These penguins spend their entire lives around the Galapagos Islands.

Emperor penguins may walk up to 75 miles (121 km) inland to reach their mating sites.

Krill

Krill are crustaceans that look like shrimp. They range in length from 0.4 to 5.5 inches (1 to 14 cm). Krill feed on phytoplankton at the surface of the water. They are found in all the world's oceans but are very important to the polar region ecosystem. Every animal species living in Antarctica depends directly or indirectly on krill. Seabirds, penguins, seals, whales, fish, and squid all feed on these creatures. The largest animal on the planet, the blue whale, eats almost nothing but krill.

Eco Facts

Krill are the most abundant animal on the planet. An estimated 500 million tons (453 million tonnes) of krill live in the Southern Ocean. Almost every animal that lives in the Antarctic is subject to the *three degrees of krill* rule: you are krill, you eat krill, or your food eats krill.

Squid

These **mollusks** are fast-swimming predators. Squid hunt by shooting out two tentacles armed with hooks or suckers to grab their prey. Squid eat crustaceans, fish, and other squid. They can also squirt a thick cloud of black ink to help them escape from predators. Most squid are no more than 24 inches (61 cm) long. The colossal squid, found in the seas around Antarctica, can grow to more than 40 feet (12 m) long and weigh up to 1,000 pounds (454 kg).

Squid can change color. This helps them attract mates.

Polar Regions in Danger

Polar region ecosystems are threatened due to climate change and human activity. Higher average temperatures have resulted in some melting of the polar ice caps. The Arctic Ocean may become ice free in summer. This would open new northern shipping routes, such as the Northwest Passage, shortening the journey between Europe and Asia. However, more shipping traffic could affect the ecosystem by introducing pollution from the ships.

There are large reserves of oil and natural gas in the Arctic. Melting ice will make these resources more accessible, and many nations are rushing to exploit them. While safeguards will be put in place, accidents can happen. Oil spills in other parts of the world, such as the Gulf of Mexico, have caused major damage to ecosystems. These ecosystems often take many years to recover.

There has been overfishing around Antarctica. Despite international agreements to protect the local fish, some species, such as the toothfish, are still being fished illegally in large numbers. Whales are now protected in the Southern Ocean. Krill, however, are still being caught in vast amounts for human consumption. This threatens many ecosystems, especially the polar regions, since animals ranging from huge whales to small fish rely on krill for survival.

Timeline of Human Activity in Polar Regions

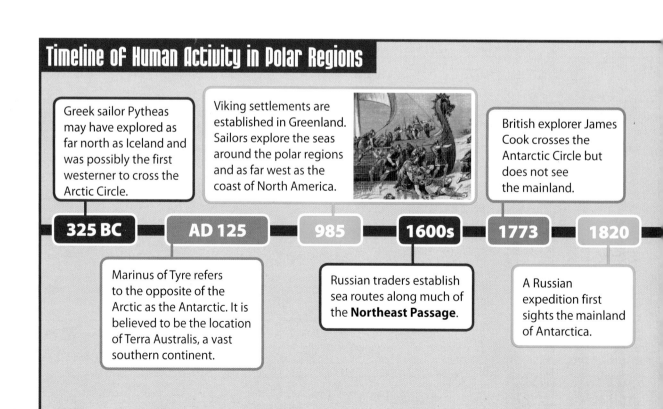

Greek sailor Pytheas may have explored as far north as Iceland and was possibly the first westerner to cross the Arctic Circle.

Viking settlements are established in Greenland. Sailors explore the seas around the polar regions and as far west as the coast of North America.

British explorer James Cook crosses the Antarctic Circle but does not see the mainland.

325 BC   **AD 125**   **985**   **1600s**   **1773**   **1820**

Marinus of Tyre refers to the opposite of the Arctic as the Antarctic. It is believed to be the location of Terra Australis, a vast southern continent.

Russian traders establish sea routes along much of the **Northeast Passage**.

A Russian expedition first sights the mainland of Antarctica.

Pollution is also a problem. Ocean currents carry pollution from populated regions to the remote polar regions. The polar regions have also experienced pollution from ships dumping garbage and toxic waste.

The ozone layer is a layer of gas in the atmosphere that blocks some of the Sun's UV rays. Too much UV harms humans, plants, and animals. Pollution has damaged this layer, creating holes over the poles. The Antarctic hole is the largest hole. Every spring, this hole grows as big as the United States. It shrinks over winter. In the Arctic, the ozone hole is smaller. At both poles, the stronger UV rays caused by the holes kill plankton that many organisms eat, which affects the food chain.

Drilling for oil requires a great deal of construction activity, such as building roads and pipelines to transport the oil. This can disrupt the ecosystem.

Explorer Robert Peary claims to be the first person ever to reach the North Pole.

Richard E. Byrd claims to be the first person to reach the North Pole by plane, although this remains in dispute.

In August, two Russian submersibles descend 13,979 feet (4,261 m) to the ocean floor under the North Pole.

1906 **1909** **1911** **1926** **1956** **2007**

Roald Amundsen becomes the first person to sail through the Northwest Passage. It takes him 3 years.

Amundsen becomes the first person to reach the South Pole.

The U.S. Navy sets up the first permanent base at the South Pole, the Amundsen–Scott South Pole Station.

Science in the Polar Regions

Arctic researchers often must perform dangerous acts, such as climbing onto icebergs.

The polar regions are important indicators of climate change. Scientists study these regions because they are easily affected by slight changes in the environment. However, due to the harsh climate, working in polar regions presents many challenges for scientists. They often must rely on tools such as submersibles to help them explore these areas. Submersibles are vehicles used by scientists to explore underwater. Some are remotely controlled, while others are operated by people. Using submersibles, scientists are able to examine areas that would otherwise be impossible to reach.

Research Bases

In the Arctic, some research bases move with the ice. Situated on glacier fragments or other large pieces of ice, these stations can move thousands of miles (km) with the ocean currents. There have been many Soviet or Russian drifting ice stations in the Arctic over the years. The Soviet Union operated 31 Arctic stations between 1937 and 1991. Russia resumed explorations of the Arctic in 2003.

Many countries also have bases in Antarctica. Unlike Arctic bases, which are built on sea ice, Antarctic research bases are built on the Antarctic continent. There are more than 30 permanent bases on Antarctica. In the summer, there can be more than 4,000 research personnel on the continent. This number drops to about 1,000 in the winter.

Animal Oceanographers

Scientists can use radio tagging to learn about animals. Researchers catch animals and attach electronic tags to them. The animals are then released. The tags send radio signals to research stations, which track the animals' movements. Tracking helps scientists learn more about the local habitat and how to better protect endangered animals and environments. In polar regions, thick ice limits the use of ships, tracking buoys, and floats. As advances in technology continue, more data can be obtained. In the Antarctic, southern elephant seals fitted with electronic sensors were recorded at depths of almost 3,000 feet (914 m).

Scientists can test pollution levels by examining the organisms in the environment.

Working in the Polar Regions

Scientists must drug polar bears before they can safely attach tracking tags.

Working in polar regions can be exciting, but it can also be dangerous. Polar bears are always a threat in Arctic regions, so scientists must use caution when working in the field. The weather is another hazard. Scientists must be prepared to spend time outside in very cold temperatures. There are many careers related to polar regions. Before considering these careers, it is important to learn the educational requirements.

Oceanographer

Duties

Studies the physical properties of the ocean, including ocean waves, currents, and geology

Education

Bachelor of science, masters, or doctoral degree in marine science

Interests

Oceanography, the environment, biology, ecology

Oceanographers analyze the currents, waves, and ocean temperatures at the polar regions. Oceanographers also study and try to predict the effects of climate change on polar waters.

Other Coral Reef Jobs

Biologist

Studies the animals that live in polar regions and how they interact with each other and their environments

Ecologist

Assesses habitats in polar ecosystems, including pollution levels

Fisheries Officer

Ensures the protection of sensitive polar region ecosystems by monitoring fishing practices and their effects on the environment

Photographer

Uses photographic equipment to document the organisms that inhabit polar region ecosystems

Roald Amundsen

Roald Amundsen (1872–1928) was a Norwegian explorer of the Arctic and Antarctic. He was the first person to travel to both the North and South Poles.

In 1887, Amundsen joined the *Belgica*, an antarctic exploration ship. The crew of the *Belgica* became the first people to spend the winter in Antarctica. On that trip, Amundsen learned valuable survival lessons that would serve him well on his future expeditions in the polar regions.

Amundsen was planning a trip to the North Pole when he learned that Robert Peary had claimed to have completed the trek. Amundsen decided to travel to the South Pole instead. This put him in a race with Britain's Robert Scott to be the first to reach the South Pole. Amundsen arrived first, in December 1911. His team had traveled more than 1,800 miles (2,900 km) in 99 days. Scott arrived at the South Pole five weeks later. Overcome by the harsh conditions, Scott and his team died on the journey back.

In 1926, Amundsen led an expedition that flew over the North Pole in the airship, *Norge*. Two years later, Amundsen died in a plane crash in the Arctic while attempting to rescue the downed crew of another airship.

Water freezes at 32°F (0° C), but salt changes the freezing point of water. It lowers it. Salty water can be colder than the freezing point and still be a liquid. Seawater is salty. Try this experiment to test the freezing point of different kinds of water.

Materials

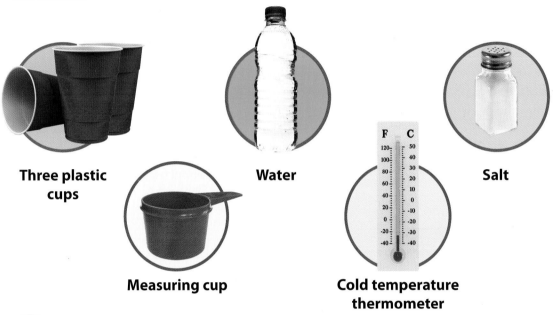

Three plastic cups

Water

Salt

Measuring cup

Cold temperature thermometer

1 Fill the cups with water.

2 In the first cup, mix a 1/4 cup (60 milliliters) of salt. In the second cup, mix 2 tablespoons (30 ml) of salt. Put no salt in the third cup. Make sure to label each cup with how much salt is in it. Clear plastic cups will give a better view of the ice forming. Glass may break, so be sure only to use plastic.

3 Put all three cups in a freezer.

4 Check the cups every 20 minutes and record your findings. If you have a thermometer, measure the temperature of the salty water. What happened to the different types of water after an hour?

Create a Food Web

U se this book, and research on the Internet, to create a food web of polar region ecosystem producers and consumers. Start by finding at least three organisms of each type—producers, primary consumers, secondary consumers, and tertiary consumers. Then, begin linking these organisms together into food chains. Draw the arrows of each food chain in a different color. Use a **red** pen or crayon for one food chain and green and blue for the others. You should find that many of these food chains connect, creating a food web. Add the rest of the arrows to complete the food web using a pencil or **black** pen.

Once your food web is complete, use it to answer the following questions.

1 How would removing one organism from your food web affect the other organisms in the web?

2 What would happen to the rest of the food web if the producers were taken away?

3 How would decomposers fit into the food web?

Sample Food Web

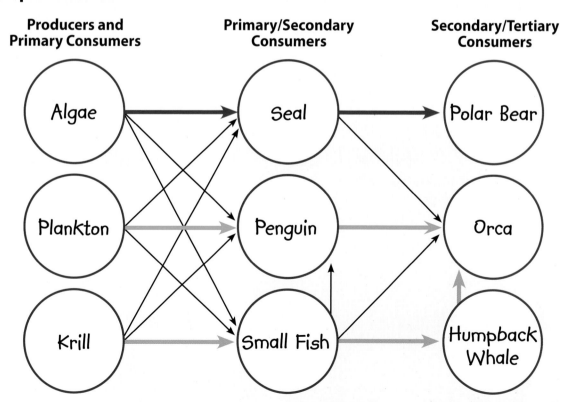

Producers and Primary Consumers	Primary/Secondary Consumers	Secondary/Tertiary Consumers

Algae, Plankton, Krill, Seal, Penguin, Small Fish, Polar Bear, Orca, Humpback Whale

1. What percentage of the Earth's fresh water is contained in the ice of Antarctica?

2. What is the coldest temperature ever recorded on Earth?

3. What is the midnight sun?

4. How much does the male Pacific walrus weigh?

5. What is the northernmost wood-producing plant in the world?

6. What is the average thickness of the Greenland ice sheet?

7. How deep did the Russian submersibles descend at the North Pole in 2007?

8. In what year did Roald Amundsen reach the South Pole?

9. How many major species of penguins live in Antarctica?

10. To what length can male orcas grow?

Key Words

atmosphere: the layer of gases, such as oxygen, that surrounds Earth

crustaceans: organisms with a hard shell to protect their boneless, soft bodies

dormant: a volcano that is not currently erupting but may do so in the future

ecosystems: communities of living things sharing an environment

hemisphere: one half of Earth

invertebrates: organisms with no backbones, or spines

latitude: imaginary lines around Earth used on maps for navigation and other purposes

magnetic field: a magnetic force that surrounds Earth and protects it from the Sun's rays

mollusks: soft-bodied invertebrates, such as snails, slugs, and octopuses

Northeast Passage: a sea route along the northern coast of Europe and Asia

Northwest Passage: a sea route along the northern coast of North America

organic: made up of living things

organisms: living things

peninsula: an area of land almost entirely surrounded by water

permafrost: soil that is at or below 32°F (0°C) for two or more years

precipitation: water that falls to Earth in the form of rain or snow

predators: animals that hunt other animals for food

species: a group of similar organisms that can mate to create offspring that can also mate

tundra: an area in a polar region where trees find it difficult to grow due to low temperatures and short growing seasons

Index

Antarctic Circle 6, 7, 9, 22
Arctic Circle 6, 7, 22
aurora borealis/aurora australis 13

climate change 5, 6, 10, 17, 19, 22, 24, 27

icebergs 6, 13, 24

magnetic field 7, 13
mammals 18
marine biologist 27

Northeast Passage 22
North Pole 4, 6, 7, 10, 11, 13, 23, 27, 30
Northwest Passage 6, 8, 22, 23

oceanographer 25, 27

penguins 6, 7, 15, 20, 21, 29, 30
polar bear 15, 18, 19, 26, 29

South Pole 4, 6, 7, 9, 10, 11 13, 23, 27, 30

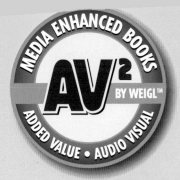

Log on to www.av2books.com

AV[2] by Weigl brings you media enhanced books that support active learning. Go to www.av2books.com, and enter the special code found on page 2 of this book. You will gain access to enriched and enhanced content that supplements and complements this book. Content includes video, audio, weblinks, quizzes, a slide show, and activities.

AV[2] Online Navigation

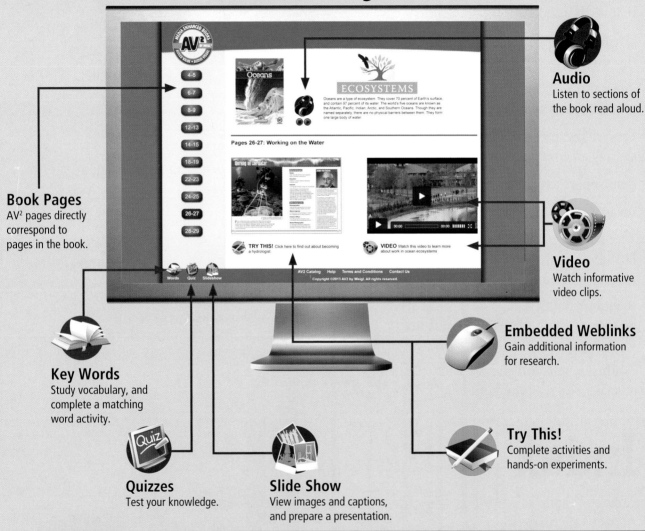

Audio
Listen to sections of the book read aloud.

Video
Watch informative video clips.

Embedded Weblinks
Gain additional information for research.

Try This!
Complete activities and hands-on experiments.

Book Pages
AV[2] pages directly correspond to pages in the book.

Key Words
Study vocabulary, and complete a matching word activity.

Quizzes
Test your knowledge.

Slide Show
View images and captions, and prepare a presentation.

AV[2] was built to bridge the gap between print and digital. We encourage you to tell us what you like and what you want to see in the future.

Sign up to be an AV[2] Ambassador at www.av2books.com/ambassador.